sundance
publishing

LITTLE RED
READERS

Jon Sleeps On

PETER SLOAN &
SHERYL SLOAN

Illustrated by Teresa Culkin-Lawrence

Jon liked to do two things:
sleep and eat ice cream.
One morning
his alarm clock rang,
but Jon went on sleeping.

"Get up, Jon.
Time to go to school,"
his mother called
as she left for work.
But Jon went on sleeping.

3

"Get up, Jon.
You will be late,"
his father called.
But Jon went on sleeping.

4

Jon's father went outside
to get the paper.
The wind blew
the door shut.
Father banged on the door.
But Jon went on sleeping.

Along came
a police officer.
She blew her whistle loudly.
But Jon went on sleeping.

A fire engine roared by
with its siren wailing.
The police officer was
blowing her whistle.
And Father was banging.
But Jon went on sleeping.

An ice-cream truck
came down the street.
The driver rang the bell.
Jon ran out of the house.
"Well, he's up now!"
laughed his father.